RIDING TO MY HEART

Hayley Richard

Contents

Meeting the Soon to Be

E xcitement pulsed through the air as everyone got ready for the rodeo ahead. The broncs were running in their pastures, the bulls were either sleeping or eating, the steers were bathing in the morning sun, and the riders and their horses were warming up in the arena. It was only 8:00 am and was already 88 degrees, for Dallas, Texas that was average. A full five days of rodeo, there are so many riders here it takes a day per event. First bronc riding, then bulls, after is tie down and break away roping, the following day come the team ropers, and finally barrels and poles on the last day. Riders were everywhere, thousands of people in the rodeo grounds, but for this story we're gonna focus on a duo of teenage girls, Skylar Jones and Elena Lane( ).

Earlier that morning 6:00am July 2ndSkylar got out of bed and fed her horse Honor, her huge bay and white paint thoroughbred. She then started cleaning her show tack. Right as Sky was stepping in the trailer's tack room Elena came out to feed Hollywood and joined Sky. "Hey Sky, there's this party tonight to kick off rodeo week. Can we go please?""Ooh that sounds like fun, yea we'll go. But absolutely no drinking. Got it?" "YES Sky I got it. Yay! Music, dancing, and boys!" "Ya boys are not on my list. But dancing with a few sounds good." After cleaning their tack they grabbed their practice tack and headed out to saddle their horses.

Levi and SawyerLevi and Sawyer fed their horses and are now tacking up to head for the arena. "Hey Sawyer we're goin to that party tonight right?" "Damn right we are!" "Awesome! Can't wait!" "Me neither." They finished saddling and headed to the arena.

At the arenaSkylar and Elena were warming up their swing while an arena worker got them a steer. When their steer finally arrived they settled into the shoots. Sky was the header and Ele the heeler. The calf was released and Sky took off swingin, she looped the head and pulled him around for Ele, she pulled in both hinds and dallied off. They both looked at their time. Record breaking! "Yea we did it!" Yelled Elena releasing the calf. "That's right Cowgirl! We're the pros!" replied Skylar giving Ele a high five. Then giving Honor a well deserved pat. "Hey nice job girls." Said Levi. Skylar turned around to see a blue eyed, handsome cowboy, on a chestnut mare next to an equally attractive guy on a red roan gelding. "Thanks! You guys a team?" "Yes we are. Best in Dallas!" Replied Sawyer. "Oh really? Can you run a time like that? Cause we're from right here in Dallas!" Yelled Elena from behind Sky. "Well...um...I didn't mean it like that."Sawyer said regaining his authoritative voice from before. "Sawyer just shut up. Stop trying to show off." Replied Levi. "Well we best be goin. I gotta start prepping for today's event."Sky said as she walked away. "Ok bye it was nice meeting you! Wait we never caught your names!" Yelled Levi "oh my name is Skylar. And that's Elena. How bout you? I know Sawyer." "My name is Levi. Yep that's Sawyer. The idiot." "I'm not that bad." "Ha sure." "Nice meetin y'all. We'll see ya round."Elena said sweetly. Ele and Sky rode away and Ele said,"Man were they hot!" "Yea but I doubt they're very nice guys." "Hey give em a chance ya never know. That Levi guy was checkin you out. Woowee it feels like 100 already!" "Yea I know it's 8:30 and we're already dying!" They headed back to their trailer and Sky got her gear ready for bronc riding. Then headed out to get her number and draw her horse, she was gonna meet back up with Ele for them to get breakfast after. The rodeo started at ten so they had plenty of time. "Howdy ma'am what can I do for you?" Drawled the man at the sign up booth. "I'm here to get my number." "Well I'm sorry to inform you barrel racin ain't till Friday ma'am." "I ain't here to sign in for barrels. And I know barrels are on Friday. And ropin is on Wednesday then I'll be with my partner on Thursday but today I ride broncs!" Sky replied a little annoyed. Having to deal with this is gettin really annoyin. She thought. "Oh I'm so sorry ma'am..." "Stop calling me ma'am. You can see I'm only round 17. Names Skylar Jones. Right there on the list. Now can I please have my number and horse so I can meet my friend for breakfast?" "Yea...um here ya go...um...Skylar?" He more asked than stated. Sky looked at her horse's name know all too well who this horse was. It was her daddy's bronc. Skylar's daddy bred broncs and bulls for rodeos. As well as run a very successful meat

cattle business. Horse's name was Knightshade, black as night and
not a speck of white on him. He was a lengthy thoroughbred with
long powerful legs and a very long neck and back. He was a monster
of a horse. Good thing I know him better'n my own brain. Thought
Skylar on her way to meet Elena at the pancake house. They got
seated quickly and ordered their favorites. "I'll take your cheesecake
bite pancakes with strawberries on the side please." Ordered Skylar.
"And I'd like your famous buttermilk pancakes with honey instead
of syrup please." "Alright I'll be right back with those." "Thanks"
Skylar smiled at the waitress. "So what horse did you get?" Elena
asked Skylar. "Knightshade" Sky replied grimly. "Oh shit! Your dead
meat!" "I know. But if I can ride him through I'm sure to win. He
has amazing bucks." "And you have amazing form!" Sky blushed
and took a drink of her coffee Elena doing the same. "Aright here
you ladies go. One short stack of buttermilk pancakes with honey
not syrup. And one short stack of cheesecake bite pancakes with
strawberries on the side. Enjoy!" "Thank you. It looks really good."
Elena and Skylar said together. They ate then walked back to the tra
iler.~~~~~~~~~Rodeo~Starts~~~~~~~~~~"Ladies and gentlemen!
Today is the start of rodeo week here in Dallas. And today we kick
it off with our bronc riders!" All the bronc riders rode out on their
own horses galloping around the arena. All the guys were looking at
Skylar as she rode proudly around the ring. She then dropped her
reins on Honor's neck and threw her hands up. What no body knew
was that she had a semi trick riding saddle on. Her practice saddle
had foot holders. Random spectator's POV There was a girl in the

group. I watched her as she dropped her reins then started to stand. She slipped her boots into some kind of foot holds. She picked up a long rein attached to her horses bridle and stood up completely. "Hey fellas lookie here! Not only do we have ourselves a girl ridin broncs but she's a trick rider as well! What next she gonna go round them barrels standin?" Everyone laughed. She then leaped out of the foot holds and back into the saddle slipping her boots into her normal stirrups all in one smooth motion. She then sat back and lightly picked up her reins at that cue her horse, which was that last in the line, sat back and slide to a stop. Everyone else stopped their horses next to her and faced the stands.Back to normal POV "You got no chance Jones. Not with you ridin Knightshade." "I'll have you know I can ride anything. I trained that horse as a two year old. I know how he works!" Sky replied mercilessly. I can't believe she rides! Levi thought in his head. "These here are our bronc riders today. Over on the far left we have Logan Ray ridin Gallant Man..." The announcer went through the riders and their horses all the way till he got to Levi. "Levi Erickson with Crown Royal..." Another one of my daddy's. Thought Skylar as they went through the horses. "And finally we have Skylar Jones riding Knightshade!" The crowd went wild at the horses name, everyone round here knows Knightshade. All the riders galloped one last lap before exiting the arena. The broncs were being gathered and put into their shoots and behind them the riders were suiting up. The first 15 riders went only 6 rode the 8. Next rides Levi and he made the 8 with great form. 12 more went then the guy who teased Sky rode and fell before he even got out the gate. When he went back behind the shoots Skylar laughed and said," Watch and learn!" She then climbed up onto the fence. Skylar's POV I climbed up and into the shoot, I sat down on Knightshade and whispered in his ear," Hey buddy! Miss me? That's right I'm back! You remember the one you couldn't throw!" When I used to talk to him like this during training it made him buck better and harder. "You ready yet Sky?" Asked my daddy's gate keeper Ryan. "Yeah yeah Ryan. Hold up." I settled back got myself situated, nodded my head and slapped Knight on the a** before he leaped and twisted out of the shoot. He tried and tried but I never faltered. The buzzer rang and I jumped off him. I ran back to the shoots and over to Elena who was waiting for me.

Narrator POVThey got Knightshade back into the pasture and 15 more riders went. Finally at 2:30 they finished with the riders and were calculating the results. Fifteen minutes later they were ready. "Alright everyone. We have our winners. In third place we have Dalton Young. In second is Levi Erickson. And in first place we have Skylar Jones!" The crowd cheered, whooped, hollered, and whistled. All the winners received their purses and their tickets to the next rodeo. "Theses three riders have qualified for the next qualifying rodeo in Austin. Sky exited the arena and ran to Ele,"You did it Sky!" "I know! I know! I did it!" They walked back to their trailer to got ready for the party.

~~~~~~~~later~that~evening~~~~~~~~After taking showers Sky and Ele went out to feed the horses. Next they went back into the "house"

and did their hair, makeup, and got dressed. They were both ready by 5:30 and decided to go to dinner. They went to the party and got some drinks, root beer for both. They then went to the dance floor and danced together waiting until someone asked them. Levi walked up to Skylar but stopped behind her and watched her dance for a second. Then asked,"Hey...um...Skylar?..." Sky turned around and smiled when she saw the blue eyed cowboy. "Hey Levi!" "Hey. I was wondering if you..." "Yes I'd love to dance with you!" "Really?" Levi asked. "Yea let's go!" Levi and Skylar danced the night away. And when the party was over Levi said,"Hey Skylar maybe we can go out to dinner sometime?" "I'm sorry Levi, I'm not looking for a relationship right now." "Oh...well then I guess I'll...see you aro und..." "Hey I don't mean never. Just not right now. I'd like to be friends though." Skylar quickly replied. "Alright. We'll be friends." He forced a smile to cover the disappointment. (Earlier; focused on Elena)Elena was dancing with Skylar when Levi came and took Sky to dance. Just after Sawyer came over and asked Ele to dance. They danced for hours then headed out to the bonfire. After an hour there they said their goodbyes, exchanged numbers and Elena went off to find Skylar. Then they both headed back to their trailer.

Party Day

J uly 3rdThe rodeo excitement still hung thick in the air, but for Skylar and Elena it was quite relaxing. The day held bull riding so they could be spectators for once. And they could attend party after party. They woke up a little later and fed the horses, then Skylar went to pick up her Queensland heeler, Cali(picture at top). They had planned to meet up with Levi and Sawyer for breakfast at the Pancake House. "What should I wear?" Elena was already dressed and was styling her jet black hair. "You? Stressing about what to wear? I thought you didn't like him?" "I never said I didn't like him. I just don't want a boyfriend right now." "Sure! Um...you should wear that pink and black button up. That one is really cute on you!" "Oh yeah I forgot bout that one! Thanks!" "Anytime! And I mean it. ANYTIME!" They finished getting ready and went to the restaurant. The boys had just gotten there and were seated when Sky and Ele arrived. "Hey girls! We're over here!" "Hey Levi, Sawyer!" Skylar greeted when they arrived at the table. "Howdy Skylar, so what do y'all have planned for the day?" Asked Levi. "Hey Elena, and same question what ya doin?" "Well we planned on being spectators today and just watch some of the bull riders. Not all though. I don't really like the bull ridin." Skylar told the boys. "Yea me neither." Added Ele. "Well there's this trail not far from here. We could all ride that!" Said Levi. "That sounds fun. I haven't been on a trail ride in forever!" Skylar said excitedly. "I'll go!" "Me too!" Ele and Sawyer replied. They all got their horses tacked and loaded up in Sawyer and Levi's four horse stock trailer.

They all headed out for the trail, when they arrived they hopped on and rode off. They were all walking along talking and laughing when someone came running through the brush with a mask on. He held up a gun at the group and yelled,"Don't none of y'all move! Ya hear?" They all nodded and stood still. Not even the horses moved and inch. Skylar's POV The man with the gun walked up to me and Honor. He leaped up onto Hon's back and aimed the gun at my head. "Y'all are gonna ride me on up near that ridge!" He said then kicked Honor. He jumped forward into a very fast walk. "Wait you can ride behind me!"Levi said. The man turned to him and replied," Oh but I'd much rather have my arms round a beautiful girl like her. I mean wouldn't you?" He chuckled then wrapped his filthy arms around my narrow waist. "Please get you hands off me. You can hold the saddle." I said calmly. "I'm the one with the gun. Now ain't I? You'll do what I say!" He said demandingly. "Yes sir." I replied quietly. "Now that's a good girl." He said while stoking my hair with his gunned hand. When I flinched he tapped me with the gun. "Don't you move when I touch you!" "Stop messing with her!" Levi yelled at him. I stayed quiet. The man stuck the gun under my jaw and said,"Another word of protest out of you and she'll get your bullet!" "Ye-yes s-sir." Levi stuttered. I looked back at Ele, I love you, she mouthed, love you more. I mouthed back and forced a smile. We finally made it to the ridge and the man said,"Ride me right up there." He pointed with the gun to a certain spot. Everyone moved forward," No only this one!" He shouted and knocked me in the head with the barrel of the gun. "Ow!" I shrieked. "Shut up!" He yelled at me and hit me again, I had already been crying for the past 5 minutes. But everyone could hear me now. I asked Honor to walk on and he did so hesitantly. "It's ok buddy walk on." I stammered. We walked up just past the ridge where he said and he got off running his hands down me as he did so. "It really is a shame." Was all he said before running to the top of the hill. I galloped back to Levi he was dismounted and I practically fell of my horse and into his arms. I was sobbing as he rubbed my back, rocking and humming.Narrator POV Honor and the other horses were grazing while Levi tried to calm Skylar. They were sitting on the ground and he was softly singing an old country love song to her while rubbing her back and rocking her gently. He layed back with her on top of him. She soon fell asleep but he kept singing. Sawyer and Elena were walking around wondering what to do. They couldn't just let him go, but they had no service all the way up here. And they weren't leaving anytime soon with Skylar's condition. They walked back to find Sky asleep on top of a singing Levi. "How is she?" Asked Sawyer. "She's better she stopped crying and shaking then just passed out." "She had it ruff. We're just lucky he didn't kidnap her when they went on a little." Ele said sadly. "Yea well

I'm gonna hold her on Jazzi. Can one of you lead Honor?" "Yea I'll take him. Him and Holly are friendly." "Thanks" Sawyer helped Levi while he got on Jazzi with Skylar. She stirred a little then went back to sleep. They walked awhile before she woke up and moved behind Levi. She was half dozing on his shoulder the whole way back to the trailer. Both girls fell asleep on their guys once in the truck and slept the whole way back to the rodeo grounds. The guys carried them into the "house" and just as they were leaving the girls both said, "No stay. I don't wanna be alone!" "We're just going to take care of the horses then we'll be back." Said Sawyer. "Ok" They all slept for two hours then got up and dressed up. There was a couple parties tonight and they were going to all of them. "Oh a dress?" Ele asked Sky. "I kinda changed my mind bout relationships." She smiled shyly. "Omg yay! Now we can go on double dates!!!" "Yea yea whatever. Let's just finish getting ready." They all met up after feeding the horses and headed off to party. _____They went to party after party, dance after dance. When ones songs got boring they moved on. None of them took a single drink though. (Skylar was impressed with everyone) They slow danced, speed danced, and danced like lunatics. They arrived at one place called the Crazy Horse, this place had a mechanical bull. When Skylar saw this she squealed. "I wanna ride it!" "Ok let's go ride it." "I'm better!" Yelled Sky as she ran to the worker. "Prove it!" Says Levi. "I will!" Replies Sky who then runs out and jumps on the beast. She throws her hand up and nods her head. It starts rocking slowly getting faster and faster until its spinning and bucking and it's unbelievable how she's staying on.

She stuck to that bull like glue, they moved as one. She wasn't comin off, there was no end. The worker took Manuel control and had it spin randomly which finally threw her. "Beat that!" She yelled. "Yea you already win." Responded Levi. "She is one with an animal, whether it be fake or real." Ele said with a smile. Everyone rode the bull then they all danced one more round and sat down at the bar. "What's one round?" Asked Skylar "Y'all got 'ids' right?" Whispered Sawyer. "Yes!" Ele, Sky, and Levi replied. They all got a beer and took one shot of whiskey. The girls took theirs straight while the guys secretly got some water. They danced and played around then the guys went to the bathroom. While the guys were gone the girls grabbed another shot of whiskey. And more beer for all of them. The boys can back and they danced another 15 mins before walking back to the trailers. "What is wrong with you guys? Your all over the place!" Elena went with Sawyer and Skylar took Levi with her. They all fell asleep quickly, but the girls confessed before they went to sleep.

Roping

Today everyone got up and ready for roping. There are two events today, both roping. The first is tie down, followed by break away. Elena and Skylar are doing both, as well as Sawyer and Levi. Elena and the guys got up late due to the late night they had. They all woke up with pounding headaches. "Ah. My brain is screaming at me!" Said Ele. "I know. But we've got to get ready for tie down its in two hours. Don't worry I already fed all the horses. So everyone get dressed." Said Sky, who woke up early despite her headache. Levi walked up and wrapped his arms around her waist, kissed her neck, and whispered, "Thank you, Sky-pie!" In her ear. Sky looked over and saw Sawyer and Elena both sleeping again. So she thought of an idea, she handed Levi two pans and got her blow horn, she also had the music player ready to play 8 Second Ride by Jake Owen full blast. "Ok on three!" She whispered. "One...two...three!" They set off all three of the loud obnoxious noises. The two sleeping love birds leaped out of the bed and then turned and glared at Sky and Levi. The two jokesters ran for their lives. They ran and Sky jumped on Honor, her huge gelding was trained for free riding, so she galloped away. She yelled at Levi to swing up, so he did and wrapped tight around her frame. They galloped over to his trailer and he saddled and bridled his horse then they went to the arena. "Let's do some circles and figure eights at a working trot." Sky said. They did 4 of each then picked up speed. "Next well do an extended trot." Levi said. Next they moved into a collected canter, then onto an extended canter, and finally a gallop. "Race you round the arena!" Sky shouted. "Your on!" Levi replied. "Ready...set...race!" They had a gate keeper start them off. The arena wasn't too large, just big enough for the barrel pattern, bout 1000m in perimeter. Skylar's POV I leaned forward and whispered ,"let's win!" In Honor's ears just before I heard "Ready...set...race!" I yelled,"Git!" And squeezed my calfs on Honor. He launched off his hindquarters and went full out. We ran and left Levi in the dust, he started out ahead cause his horse was the equivalent to a 400m sprinter while mine was the equivalent to a 800m sprinter. We were baring down on the finish line, Levi and Jaz were starting to catch up so I asked Honor for one last surge. We crossed the finish line first and I threw my hands up, while sitting back asking Honor to slow. "I win!" "Yea I know you don't have to rub it in!" Levi joked. We walked the horses out and headed back to the trailers. Narrator POV Sky and Levi cooled their horses out and put them in their stalls. Then they went into the "house" part and got dressed for the event. Sky wore a blue pearl snap. Elena wore a light sea foam green pearl snap. Levi wore a black and red button up, and Sawyer wore a white button up. They all went out and groomed the horses then clean their tack and saddled up. They went over and trotted round the arena until the announcer called to clear the arena. He started calling names of riders to enter the ring for the line up. The event started off with a bang, quite literally it was Fourth of July and they just set of a row of fireworks. After that the announcer called the first rider and the first steer was loaded. Multiple riders went before any of the group was called. The first of the four was Elena. She backed into the corner and when the steer was released she took in after it. She roped and tied it up in 8s, she was the leader so far. A couple more riders went then Levi was called. He got 8.23s second place holder. After one more rider Sawyer was called. He tied up in 8.9. The very last rider was Skylar. She rode in lined up and caught her steer dismounted and flipped her steer then went to tie up the feet and as she finished the knot one foot can loose. The run was disqualified. "Ah damn it!" Sky yelled when she exited the arena. "Well there goes roping for the season! Damn it!" Levi's POV I knew Sky was mad so I went over just to be with her. I wasn't gonna be all sappy she doesn't like that. I'll just be matter of fact with her. If she needs I'll be her shoulder, her anything. I walk over to her, she is already off her horse praising him for his job well done. She ties Honor up at the water trough when she sees me and comes running into my arms. "It'll be alright. Sorry bout that run." "Don't apologize. It wasn't your fault I should have had a better grip and pulled the knot before I took my hands off." "Let's take Honor back to the trailer and take a little break before break away, alright?" I asked her. "Ok" was all she said. We met Sawyer and Elena back at the trailer for lunch. "Hey guys what's for lunch?" Sky yelled out. She wasn't one to stay upset long, or at least show it long. Soon enough she'll of had too much pent up and I'll be here for her when she finally breaks down her walls. We had grilled cheese sandwiches and a small fruit bowl. And when we heard the call for break away we cleaned up, tacked up, and rode back to the arena. Narrator POV They did the line up again then started the event. This time Sawyer was the first of the group to be called, he was the fifth rider total. He got a run of 4s "a little slow out the gate" he said to the squad afterwards. After ten riders they called Elena. She rode a 3.47s and had first place. Five more then Levi was called. He roped the steer and sat back looking at the clock he saw 3.46s. "Sorry Lane but your gonna have to be a tad faster next time. Like two hundredths of a second to be exact." Levi smiled and joked with Elena. Next was Skylar. She lined up and when the cue came exploded out the shoot. She threw her loop and got both horns, she sat back cueing Honor to do the same. She looked back at the clock, 2.1s. "Thank the lord!" She yelled right there. "Folks that's an arena record, you've got yourself an extra $100 here Skylar Jones." The announcer boomed. The rest of the riders went and the final rundown was Sky, Levi, Ele. They got their purses and tickets then went to change for the 4th of July party tonight and eat dinner. "Omg I know exactly what I'm gonna wear!" Ele said excitedly during dinner. "Same here!" Sky said in the same tone. After they all finished eating they went and got dressed. Ele wore a red, white, and blue fireworks shirt with some shorts that had red, white, and blue and a pair of 4th of July boots. Skylar wore an American flag shirt and shorts with some fringed festive boots. (Outfits below)

They were all ready and headed to the party.

The party lasted hours, of dancing, drinking singing, and now it's time for fireworks. "Omg! I love fireworks!" Said Ele excitedly. "I love the sight. But they're a little loud." Sky said. "Hey girlies, I got a blanket over on the grass let's go sit." Sawyer yelled from the field. They all headed over and lied down on the blanket. Elena's POV The fireworks started and were amazing! And laying in Sawyers arms was amazing as well. I smiled to myself, thinking about our lives right now. Traveling the rodeo circuit, loving boyfriends, wonderful horses, and the greatest best friend. I was just falling asleep as the fireworks ended. Skylar's POV The fireworks were beautiful, way too loud but super pretty. I was laying on Levi's chest between his legs. I fell asleep immediately after the fireworks stopped. I was in a half sleep and felt when Levi lifted me up and carried me to the truck. We drove home, me still asleepish, and Levi took off my jeans, then lied down next to me. I fell completely asleep.

Runnin With A Partner

Team roping I am so excited to finally start roping with Elena. We've been practicing for months and we can now be a team. "Skylar! We've got to get dressed! What shirt are you wearing? We've got to match!" Elena yelled at me. "I don't know! Hold on and I'll come look."

"How about this?" I asked holding up our black lace pearl snaps.

"Perfect!" We both got dressed and put sweat shirts over our shirts to keep them clean while we groomed and tacked but when we came out we found our boyfriends mounted on horses leading our perfectly groomed and tacked horses. We threw our jackets back in the trailer and hopped on our horses heading for the arena. Narrator POV Everyone got warmed up and the announcer started calling the line up, the riders entered the arena as their names were called. The first riders were called, " Skylar Jones, the header, riding Honor. And Elena Lana, the healer, riding Hollywood Runner!" They backed into their corners and when the steer was released they bolted forward. Sky looped the head tied it up and pulled it around for Ele. Elena threw her heal shot, pulled up and got both back feet she tied it up and they looked at the time. 6.253s. "We got this no doubt about it!" Elena said. "Omg I CANT believe it!!!" They headed back to the guys, who gave them hugs and kissed them before hearing their own names and lining up in the corners. They got a time of 7.251s. "Nice guys you should have second." Ele said supportively. "Thanks Boo Boo! Let's head over and grab a drink." They went over and got a drink, while Sky and Levi took their horses back to the trailer and took a nap.

A couple hours later and it was time for the awards. "Ladies and gentlemen our top three finalist teams are, drum roll please!" The crowds feet roared. "In third place we have Gertrude Hernandez riding Firework and Daren Finch riding Astro!" The crowd went wild. "In second we have Levi Erickson riding Jazzi and Sawyer Reed riding Bullseye!" Again the crowd screamed. "And in first...we have...SKY LAR JONES RIDING HONOR AND ELENA LANE RIDING HOLLYWOOD RUNNER!" It was surprising the crowd was even people they were so loud. Everyone received their rewards and went off to get ready for the parties.

"Hey guys were taking you out to dinner tonight. So dress nice." Sawyer said to the girls. "Ok we will." The girls got dressed in nice dresses.

The girls waited for the boys to pick them up. When the boys arrived they would not tell hen where they were going. "Come on Sawyer. Please tell!" "No way. It's a surprise." They drove to Logan's Road

House and got seated. "What do you want Skylar?" Levi ask. "I was thinking if you wanted to we could share somethin." "That sounds great Levi, how bout the ribs?""Great! Sawyer, Ele, what are y'all ordering?""I think I'm gonna get the mini burgers." Sawyer answered. "I'm gonna get a steak. That's what their famous for!"The waitress came and took their orders. They also received their drinks. All root beer. "You girls excited for tomorrow?" Sawyer asked. "I'm excited, nervous, freaking out, but confident." Replied Elena. "Wow Ele. Little mixed up there." Skylar said laughing. "Yea" "What about you Sky?" Levi asked. "I'm fine." She said calmly, not meaning a single word. Inside she was freaking out. Her worst enemy would be there. Dalia Rhodes. She would do anything to win, ANYTHING...Levi thinking I know something is bothering her but I don't know what. Could it be the barrel race tomorrow? Maybe someone is going to be there. I'm gonna have to find out. I'll listen to her closely and see if she gives it away subtly. Narrator POV They all received their food and ate their dinner in comfortable silence. After everyone finished eating they hall headed off to the dance.

"May I have this dance?" Sawyer asked Elena. "Yes you may!" She giggled back. They went off to dance to the slow song just coming on."Sky would you dance with me?" "I would love to!" They also went off to dance. After hours of dancing the four went home. They got the horses comfortable in their stalls, locked up the tack room, then started getting ready for bed. "Dibs on showering first!" Yelled Skylar. "Dang it!" Responded Sawyer and Elena in sync. "Not if I beat you there!" Levi announced. But Skylar was already at the door.

"Gonna have to be a little faster bae!" She said before slipping in. After everyone showered and got their pjs on they crawled into bed and immediately fell asleep.

Competion Is Rough

F RIDAY

    Barrel racing! The last day of rodeo. Tonight will be the huge awards ceremony, and after a huge dance in the arena with live music.

Again Skylar was the first one up, but Elena was up before Sky got her coffee. "Hey Ele how'd you sleep?" "Fantastic next to Sawyer." "Haha same here! Just Levi!" "Haha! Wanna go feed the horses while the coffee heats up?" "Yea sure let's go!" "So you nervous?" Ele asked Sky. "I'm dying from my nerves. Dalia Rhodes is going to be racing again!" "Ah I hate that girl!" "Yea I know. So do I!" They conversed while mixing grains and throwing hay to all four horses. When they were finished they headed back in to find two freshly made coffee cups on the table, and the guys drinking their coffee at the table. "Aw thanks guys just what I needed!" Ele said happily. Sky walked over, sat down, and stuck her head in her hands and sighed. "What's wrong Sky?" Levi asked. "What! Oh nothing!" She stood up downed her coffee and went to get dressed. She threw on her clothes as fast as she could and ran outside before anyone could question her.

Skylar's POV I got Honor tacked and headed to the arena. I wanted to make sure he was good on his feet. I was always very careful on barrels, making sure the ground was alright, and that Honor wasn't limping. My reason for being so uptight on racing day is the same reason my mother isn't here to watch me carry on in her footsteps. My mom died while running a barrel race. Flashback"Go mommy go!" "Ladies and gentlemen next up we have Maylia Skylar Jones riding Pride and Joy! This little lady has a good reputation for making all the other girls eat her dust! Alright May get it on!"She flew out of the shoot heading for the first barrel. She made the first turn perfectly at this point she would make the world record. Next I remember is everything went into slow motion and there was no sound around my. I had tunnel vision and all I could see was my mom falling right for the barrel head first. Her horses leg had hit the other causing her knee to snap, then causing her to fall throwing my mom to the barrel. She hit her head, it looked like she had broke her neck, little did I know she had shattered her spine and skull. She was pronounced dead at the scene as well as Honors dam, Joy. End of flashbackI warmed him up then moved lightly to the pattern. He turned perfectly with great form. After a little more we went back to the trailers. I unsaddled him and gave him a treat, then went into the trailer. I can't do this anymore! I just can't handle it! I need to be with you mom!Narrator POV "Skylar what are you doing!"Levi walked into the trailer to find Skylar just about to cut her wrists.

"Sky!" He ran up and grabbed the knife tossing it into the sink. "NO STOP! WHAT ARE YOU DOING!" She kept screaming. "I am here for you, Sky." He pulled her into a hug even though she fought it and ended up not hugging him back but curling into his arms and there she cried. All the years of built up and left over feelings of her mother's death and her father's abuse all flooding out. Levi started singing one of her favorite songs by Dustin Lynch, She wants a cowboy. He also rubbed her back and gently rocked her and kissed her forehead repeatedly. She soon fell asleep and was breathing evenly again. Sawyer and Elena came in and when they saw Sky's tear soaked face they had questioning looks on their faces. "Will you guys get her horse ready please?""Yea certainly. No problem, is she ok?" Sawyer asked. "Yea she's alright. I haven't got a word out of her only tears and gen she fell asleep. Sooo..." "Ok, come on Sawyer let's get the beasties ready!" Elena's POV Sawyer and I went out and got the horses out. They didn't have to worry bout theirs today so they were helping us girls out. "I wonder what is wrong with Sky." Sawyer said his voice laced with worry. "She gets like this before every barrel race. She's never actually cried before but she comes really close every time." I replied also a bit concerned. "What has she been through? I wonder?" I knew the bare minimum of her reasons but it wasn't my place to tell so I just shrugged and went on grooming. Skylar's POV I woke up with a headache but I was in Levi's arms so everything was great. We must've partied really hard last night. I thought to myself. Then everything came back to me, Levi pulling me into a hug, me breaking down and crying then falling asleep just like I am right now. He helped me so much just doing what he did, he saved me. I don't know what I was thinking, I just couldn't handle the loss with out someone to talk to. Well more like someone to MAKE me talk! I thought. Then I smiled, he loves me, he really loves me! I closed my eyes again not caring at all that the barrel race was very soon. I then felt him stir, he moved a bit and positioned him self close to my neck. So close I could feel his breath, it gave me he good kind of chills. He kissed my neck a couple times then whispered,"I know your awake." I smiled. Then he got serious but soft. "So what was all that about?" "It's my mother, she died while barrel racing and it's just very hard not having her with me. Then my father went into an aggressive depression. He beat me and locked me in a closet for days with one small drink a day." I thought back to those days and shuddered. *Flashback*"Skylar Jones! Get down here! Now!""Coming daddy!" I ran down the stairs. It was scary when daddy was angry. I wondered what I did. "Yes dadd...""What the hell is this!" He pointed where I might have spilled a little milk when eating my cereal. "Um...I might have spilled when I was eating my cereal...but I'll clean it up right now!" I ran and grabbed paper towels and started wiping the counter. "You know I have company coming today and you leave a mess like that?!? That is not aloud in MY house! IN!" He pointed to the open closet. "Please daddy! Not the closet! I'll be more careful next time! I'm really really sorry! Please daddy!" I begged but he just grabbed my arm, threw me in the closet and slammed the door. "I know you will next time, because your getting the punishment of his time!" He yelled at me then walked away, he wouldn't come back for two days. At least I got breakfast this time. *end flashback*"I am so sorry Sky. But that's all over now. You have great friends. A magnificent horse! And me. We all love you very much. Skylar. I love you." He looked me straight in the eyes and they had a glow in them I knew he meant it. "I love you too Levi. And I know. I don't know what happened today. But I'm glad you were here." I snuggled closer into him. "I'll always be here." He said into my hair.

Narrator POV "Ladies and gentlemen, our barrel racers!" All the riders galloped one lap around the arena. "Ok today y'all were gonna get right to there action! Up first we have Maybell Sanders on Friday Night."Ten rides went by. "Now is Elena Lane riding Hollywood Runner!" Elena ran perfectly around all three barrels then raced home. 14.999s ladies and gents. Fantastic ride cowgirl!" "Nice ride Elena!" All her friends greeted her right out the gate. "Skylar you made it!" Elena said excitedly. "I wouldn't miss it for the world!" Sky smiled brightly. "I'm gonna have a hard time beating that time!" Sky giggled. "Yea beat that!" Ele joked. "Riding next is Dalia Rhodes riding Nightcap." Dalia rode with a 15.1s. "And finally we have Skylar Jones riding Honor!" She ran around all three turning with perfect form and making great time. She flew home crossed the timers and let out a big deep breath. "Ladies and gentlemen we have our first tie in 17 years. Last time we had a tie this fast was when Maylia Jones and Fiona Heart both ran 15.000s. Elena Lane and Skylar Jones come out here please!" "Girls would you like to keep this a tie or have a race off?" "TIE!" Both girls yelled!"Omg this is hilarious I love it!" Ele exclaimed.

" I know right!"After they ran poles. Elena won first while Skylar got a very close second.

They all went back to the trailers to change for the awards, celebrations, and other festivities.

They got the following awards. Skylar: All around cowgirl queen won a saddle and sweatshirt. She also got individual buckles for each event she won along with a cash prize. A large cash prize. Elena: All around cowgirl princess won a bridle and breast color set and sweatshirt. Plus individual buckles as well. And also a large cash prize. Levi: All around cowboy king won saddle and sweatshirt. Individual buckles and a large cash prize. Sawyer: All around cowboy prince won bridle and breast collar set and sweatshirt. Individual buckles and a large cash prize. After awards the girls went back to change into their dresses.

The guys got in their truck and grabbed the girls once they were done dressing. They drove to where the rodeo dance was being held. They escorted their ladies to the dance floor and asked for the first dance, to the song She wants a cowboy by Dustin Lynch(the same song Levi sung to Skylar to calm her down earlier).

They danced their last night in Dallas away. They finally got back to the trailer at 3 am and went to sleep. The girls slipped their dresses off and threw on one of their boyfriends' shirts. Then they all went to sleep. They had a long drive ahead of them.

New Rodeo, New Town, Same Boys

They had been on the road for 6 hours. Going from Dallas to Amarillo. When they got there they parked the trailer and got everything situated. The girls had stayed up to make it fair to the guys, no matter how much the guys protested they didn't go to sleep. Now they all went into a deep sleep after caring for the horses. Skylar called Cali to come sleep with her. The next morning, 5:00am, Skylar got up and got some running clothes on. Then she called Cali to come with her, "Cali! Come on girl!" She whisper yelled as to not wake the others, she failed. "What ya doin babe?" Levi asked. "I'm just goin on a little run." "Can I come?" "Sure! Let's go!" "Do we get coffee first?" "No coffee after the run!" "Ugh fine!" Levi got up and got some sport shorts on and a muscle shirt. Levi, Skylar, and Cali went outside after making a water bottle. They set the bottle on the finder and started stretching. They did a quick warm up then took off. "So how far do you normally run?" Levi asked out of breath after about only five minutes. "I normally run about two miles, except when I've got something on my mind. Then it turns into five." "Dang!" Can we make it one today?" "Yea cause I haven't ran in a week so it'll only be

one. Tomorrow it will be one and a half!" "Ok sounds great!" (Back
to the trailer) Elena got up to find the coffee pot already started so she
went to check the horses. Darn not fed yet. She thought to herself.
She gave the horses hay and got their grains. She then went inside
for some coffee. After she made some pancakes, sausage, and eggs.
"Hey baby." Sawyer whispered in her ear after wrapping his arms
around her from behind. "Are you making my favorite?" "I am I am."
She smiled. "Good because I was getting hungry." "You just woke
up!" "Hey I smelled food and got hungry so I got up." He smiled
innocently. When Sky and Levi got back Sky fed Cali then they all sat
down for the breakfast Elena cooked. The rodeo wouldn't be until
tomorrow it was only two days compared to the rodeo week they
were just at. They would hold broncs, bulls, tie down, and breakaway
roping on the first day then team roping, barrel racing, and pole
bending on the second day.

"Let's go Honor we've got this!" Sky shouted and smiled. Skylar
and Elena were practicing the barrels while the guys were over by
the calf dummy working on their swings. "What was my time?" Sky
asked while leaning back, stopping Honor after their run. "14.572s"
"Alright! We got this! Good boy Honor!"

The night before the rodeo"Let's watch a scary movie!" Elena said.
"Yea! Lets do it!" Skylar exclaimed. "Um I don't know if that's such a
good idea the night before our big rodeo." Levi replied. "Yea knowing
y'all you won't sleep at all." "Just one? Please!" Elena and Skylar said
at the same time. They looked at each other and laughed. "Fine!"

Sawyer and Levi also jinxed. They looked at each other as well, but with shock instead of humor.

They decided on the movie Lights Out. (I am not going to spoil anything for those who want to watch it) This movie is about a ghost that kills people but can't be in the light for certain reasons related to when she was alive.

"Oh that was the BEST movie ever!" said Elena excitedly. "I know it had a pop up within the first five minutes!" "Alright girlies time for bed!" Levi stated. "Alright fiiinnneee." Sky drawled. They all got in their own beds to go to sleep.

IN LEVI'S ROOM(Skys POV)I couldn't sleep. I felt like someone was watching me, so I got up and crept into Levi's room. (Levi's POV) I was just about to pass out when I heard my door open. It was pitch black so I couldn't see the person who entered, but they also couldn't see my eyes were wide open. Cali leaped into my bed, scaring the crap out of me. "Crap Cali! What did you get scared?" I laughed and got up to close the door. When I lied back down I felt a person in my bed. It was a girl, Skylar, I could recognize the feeling of her soft hair. It was thick but so smooth even when she didn't brush it. I curled up next to her and wrapped hair in my arms. She just moaned in response. "Mmmmm" "Did my little Sky Pie get scared?" "Mmmmhhhhmmmm" "Well ok then you can sleep with me." I said sarcastically. "I know!" She said while rolling on top of me. I laughed. "Your cute you know that?" "Yes I do!" She smiled. She then brought herself up closer to my face, her lips hovered right above mine. "I love you." She said softly. "I love you too Sky Pie." She looked me deep in the eyes. She had a look in her eyes. I knew what she was thinking, but I could also tell she wasn't sure. She was really good at hiding her emotions from her eyes but at this moment she was an open book to me. I decided for her and closed the gap between us. She accepted the move and kissed me back passionately. (Skylar's POV)After our first kiss, my FIRST KISS, we snuggled together and fell asleep. I have never felt so safe.

30 mins earlier IN SAWYER'S ROOM(Elena's POV)I couldn't fall asleep for the life of me! I sore I kept seeing her in the dark corners of my bedroom. There was a noise threat scared me so bad A ran out of my room and jumped into Sawyer's bed. "Hey babe what's wrong?" "I heard something in my room!" I responded. (Sawyer's POV)I felt Ele jump in beside me like she was running away from something. She was probably scared because of that movie. "Hey babe what's wrong?" I asked. "I heard something in my room!" She responded then buried her head in my bare chest. I pulled her closer and rubbed her back. "Your safe now. Don't worry." "I know the movie was fake but it still scares me." "It's fine BooBoo. Just sleep." I said that but she rolled on top of me. "But I can't sleep thinking about her. I need something else to get her off my mind. " she smiled and winked at me. "Well I just might be able to fix that." I smirked. I leaned in and kissed her deeply. She immediately kissed back and wrapped her arms around my neck. She ran her fingers roughly through my hair. We broke off for a breath. "I love you Sawyer." She said in my ear.(Elena's POV)"I love you Sawyer." I whispered in his ear after breaking off the

kiss. I waited for his response but it didn't come. He pushed me from atop him and rolled over facing away from me. I decided to let it be so I just got comfy and fell asleep.

In the morningEveryone woke up and was rushing to get ready for the rodeo. They all got dressed and went out to tack the horses. The first event was bull riding. After bull riding was over it was time for broncs. Skylar, Levi, and Sawyer headed behind the shoots. Elena followed to watch. "First up we have Jacob Falterman riding Silent Killer. This stud has some wild moves on him. We'll see what this new comers got." Ooh he's kinda HOT! Elena thought to herself. Jacob rode SK with no problems. The buzzer went off. A few more riders went. "Next up we have Sawyer Reed riding Poker Face." "Good luck Sawyer!" Ele screamed. "He looked at her funny then got settled in the shoot. (Sawyer's POV)I settled into the shoot and nodded my head. Poker Face took off hard, he did a switch back that I wasn't ready for. I fell off to close to the fence. "Ahhh" I yelled after slamming my head and shoulder into the metal fence. I walked out of the arena to meet Elena. "Babe are you ok?!" "It's all your fault!" "What? My fault? How is this my fault?!?" She yelled at me. "You distracted me from my ride!" "All I said was good luck!" "I'm talking about last night!" "What about it? Our kiss? You kissed me!" "No! What you said!" "I love you?" "Yes!" "What you don't love me?" "NO I NEVER DID!" "Well...well...then you can just leave... AND DONT TOU EVER COMEBACK!!!!!" I stomped off in search of Lucy. Elena's POV I ran off blindly crying. I can't believe what just happened. He never loved me. I ran into something hard. When I looked up it was Jacob.

"Hey there darlin, what's the matter?" He asked in a deep southern accent. "My...my boyfriend just broke up with me. He...he said he never loved me." "Oh darlin I'm so sorry. It'll get better. Don't you fret. If you ever need a shoulder I'm here. Here's my number darlin." He handed me a piece of paper. "Ok thank you." He walked off leaving me in a trance. "Next up we have Levi Erickson, riding Black Jack!" I headed back to watch my friends ride. Levi and Skylar both rode well. In first place we have our new comer Jacob Falterman with 96.74 points. In second we have Skylar Jones with 94.79 points. And in third we have Levi Erickson with 90.38 points!" Narrator POV "Dang it! That dang new comer beat me!" Skylar complained. "Yea he bumped me into third!" Continued Levi. They all went back to the trailer to get their horses ready."Ladies and gentlemen! It is time for tie down roping. Can we have our cowboys and cowgirls get ready please. Up first we have Sawyer Reed riding Bullseye." Wooohooo! Go Sawyer. Win it for me babe!" Lucy yelled from the stands. Sawyer roped his steer in 3.24s. As he exited the arena he winked and waved at her. "Next up we have Jacob Falterman riding Cowboy Magic." "Go Jacob!" Elena yelled. After a few more riders Levi went. Following Levi was Elena. Now it is Skylar's turn. "Our final rider is Skylar Jones riding Honor!" Skylar took off after the steer and had him tied is 2s flat. "That puts Skylar in the lead followed by Jacob Falterman who is tied with Levi Erickson for second. In third we have Sawyer Reed and Elena Lane. Wow another tie!" "Hey Elena!" Jacob yelled. "Yea?" Ele walked over to where Jacob was. "Would you like to hang out tonight. To celebrate?" "I would love that!" "Ok I'll see you at the crazy horse at

7:00?" "Alrighty! Can I invite my friends?" "Yea of course!" Everyone went back to the trailers to get ready. It was 5:30.

Trust Me With Your Heart

7:00pm

I am really excited to hang out with Elena. From the first time I saw her bright eyes I loved her. I have always watched her ride(not like a stalker) she knows a horse so well. I hope she wants to be more than just friends. There she is! She just entered the club with her squad and damn is she looking good!

"Hey there Jacob!" "Hey Elena!" "These are my friends Skylar..." "Nice to meet you!" I accepted the hug she offered. "...and Levi." "Nice seein you again!" He smiled his real smile. "Yea it's been a while, hasn't it?" I said. "You two know each other?" Elena asked surprised. "Yea we were neighbors as kids. It's probably been ten years." I answered "Yea just about. Nice seein ya bud." "Yea. So how's the love life going now? Better'n it was back the I would hope!" I laughed. "Actually I have a beautiful, smart, amazing girl. And she rides like a pro!" "Really?! Why didn't you invite her?" "I did." He had a smirk on his face. "Well where is she?" "Right here!" He wrapped his arm around Skylar's waist and pulled her next to him. "Oh. Well you have finally gotten the girl haven't you? Well I'm real happy for ya man!" "So what about you Jacob?" "Nope I'm single and ready to mingle! But I'm definitely not going to let any of them buckle bunnies near me and my horses. I want a girl who can RIDE and ENTERS the events." "That's my girl Sky alright." He kissed her before she went off with Elena. (Elena's POV)Omg he wants someone like me!!!! I have to talk to Sky! "Sky can you come with me please!" ("That's my girl Sky alright.") She nodded and slipped out of Levi's arms. "Wait!" He gave her a kiss and we walked off."What's up?" She asked. "Soooo..." I started talking really fast."Me and Sawyer broke up earlier that's why all his stuff was gone, and I think I kinda like Jacob, I don't wanna get hurt again, and I don't know if I can trust a guy right now, but I also think Jacob is so sweet and caring and he says he wants a girl like me, I mean not exactly said that but close enough right?" I ended it all with a little question. "Whoa there girlie. Slow it down. You and Sawyer broke up? This morning? And your already into another guy?" "Yes we broke up, this morning. And I don't know!" Uuggghhh I sighed. "Well I'm really sorry about Sawyer. But I knew he was a player from the beginning, I could tell he wasn't ready for commitment." "Well why didn't you say anything?!?" "Because you were so happy. And when I saw how you two acted I thought maybe I was wrong for once. Guess not." We got drinks for the guys and ourselves then headed back to the guys. When we were walking back we heard a commotion. As we got closer we could hear it was a fight. "I wonder who's fighting!" Sky said. We looked in at the two men punching each other's lights out. The two men were Sawyer and Jacob. Jacob was just protecting his face while Sawyer was on top of Jacob punching him repeatedly. "SAWYER STOP! RIGHT NOW!" He looked up at me just before throwing his next hit.

"Sawyer what are you doing?!" "He was talking crap bout how sexy you were!" "What you think I'm not?!" "Well...no...I just don't want other people to say that about you." "You and me..." I pointed at him then me."...are o-v-e-r over!" I said. "Well...I...um I didn't mean anything I said earlier." "Yea sure. Right. I'm not fallin for it! Get out of my life!" He walked out of the bar with a red head on his arm. "Hey are you ok Jacob?" I asked while helping him up. "Yea I'm fine." I took him to a stool and got a wet rag and started wiping his brow. He had a cut there. "I'm sorry bout Sawyer..." I said. "Ahh it's fine. I can take a hit any day for you." "Well I don't want you to have to take a hit for me." I replied. "How about we get this party started!" "Yea!" Skylar had just walked up and yelled. (Narrator POV)They partied till 10 then headed back to the rodeo grounds. "Bye Jacob! I'll see you tomorrow!" Elena gave Jacob a hug. "See you tomorrow!" He answered. "Elena!" Skylar nudged Ele. Elena ran up to Jacob. " Jacob wait!" "Yea?" She jumped into his arms and kissed him. "Wow wasn't expecting that!" Skylar laughed to Levi.

The next morning "Good morning ladies and gentlemen! We're goin ta start the day off with team ropin! Let's get this rodeo started!" "Let's go Ele! I've already got Holly tacked up for you!" "Ok I'm coming!" "Sawyer I've already told you we're not a team anymore. So leave please." Levi talked calmly but strongly. Sawyer kicked dirt onto Levi's boots and walked off. "Hey there Jacob! You ready?" "Yea I'm nervous as hell but ready!" "Who isn't nervous?" They both laughed. "What you two laughin bout over there?" Skylar asked suspicious. "Jacobs a nervous reck!" Levi shouted to the girls. "Who isn't?" answered Ele. "That's why we're laughing!" "Aright guys we gotta go! Like now!" Sky yelled as she took off on Honor."First up we have Dalia Rhodes riding Nightcap and Sawyer Reed riding Bullseye." They rode and didn't get a very good time. Next, after a few riders, was Levi and Jacob. They got a time of 8.4s. "Yes! Beat that!" Said Levi. "Oh we will pretty boy we will." Skylar ran her finger along Levi. And right before they kissed she took off galloping. "Better luck next time bud." Elena said before galloping away herself. The girls ran a time of 5.7s! "Ok you can have that kiss now." She leaned in. "Just kidding!" She started laughing. Levi put a fake look of sadness. "Aw does the baby wanna real kiss?" "Just a puny, tiny, itsy, YES of course I want one!" He pulled her close and got his kiss. "Demanding much? I like it!" She whispered the last part in his ear. "Nice job Ele!" Jacob gave her a hug. "Do you mind?" "Not at all!" Again she jumped in his arms, this time he kissed her first. "Next we have poles. Come on out ladies!" Elena got first with Skylar right behind her. Dalia got third. "Finally we have barrel racing. Let's hear it for our ladies!" The crowd cheered, whistled, and screamed. First up we have Dalia Rhodes on Nightcap." Lots of riders went and now is Elena. "Next up is Elena Lane riding Hollywood Runner!" She ran 15.9s!More riders and..."Finally we have Skylar Jones riding Honor!" (Sky's POV)We can through the gate at half speed but by the time we got to the first barrel we were running thirty five. "Take a good seat and a very firm grip! Cause your in for quite a trip! He'll hit the first running thirty five. When he turns he'll seem to dive." Sit, look, turn!"Now your baring down on the second can. It's not easy as your about to learn. If you ride him through his second turn." Check, look, ask! " now your headed for number three!" Drive, drive drive! "When he leaves there set him free!!!!" I drove him all the way down the ally. I pulled him up at the end and leapt into Levi's arms. "I can feel it! We had to of won!" "I'm...I'm...I'm so proud of you!!!! Skylar you ran 14s flat!" "Oh my god oh my gosh I can't believe it!""Girl! We're going to the NFR!!!!" Elena and Skylar we're jumping like school girls. "Well it's off to the next three rodeos for some money. Then we're all goin to the NFR!" They all ran back to the trailer and put their horses away. While everyone else was making dinner Skylar snuck off into the horse stalls. "Hay buddy! How are ya? You did very good today! Your taking me and you to our moms dream! They may not have made it but we will! We will bud!" She hugged him and gave him a carrot. "Sleep tight bug!" She kissed him and ran back inside. (Back in trailer just as Sky was sneaking out)Elena was cooking and Jacob was messing with her. "Jacob stop it I'm cooking. I'm gonna splat his all over you!" "Mmmm that'd taste good!" She was making mac'n'cheese. "You'd be cleaning up the mess!" "Is help!" Levi shouted from the office. "Yea I bet you would." Ele laughed. After dinner they all went to bed early. Jacob gave Elena a goodnight kiss and left for the night. Skylar snuck into Levi's room for the second night in a row. They would be off for Mew

Mexico in the morning.Preview for the next few chapters:Elena and Jacob start dating. Sawyer doesn't like that. He also doesn't like that he isn't goin to the NFR with them, or at all for that matter. He starts sabotaging the group. First he messes with tack. Would he hurt one of the horses? Will he go as far as to hurt one of the guys or even Elena? Skylar didn't have a break down before barrels! Is Levi helping her recover? Will she have another episode before the NFR? Guess we'll find out.

Four Corners Part One

Today is Elena and Skylar's birthday but the guys don't know. Or do they? They arrived in Albuquerque, New Mexico early this morning. The guys went to "feed the horses". What they were really doing was setting up a surprise party for the girls.

"They're going to be so mad when they find out we didn't tell them our birthday was today." Ele said to Skylar. "Well I know how they are and they'll throw a huge party because it's our 18th." "Well maybe a big party isn't a bad thing?" "If you want a big party you can tell them. But I don't want a lot of people. If we tried to throw one at the club everyone in there would join." "Well I'm gonna tell them." "Alright go ahead." Elena walked out to where the boys were "feeding the horses". She opened the feed room door in the trailer and found them putting up streamers and banners. "Oh guys!" "Oh um Elena. Your not supposed to see this yet!" Jacob jumped. "How did you guys know?" "We just do!" Levi laughed. Later that morning they were finished decorating. They would throw the party after the rodeo. This was a one day rodeo that started at 10:00 am. "Ladies and gentlemen! Welcome to the 50th anual Mt. Pleasant Rodeo Round Up! We will start off with our bull riders, followed by our bronc riders, then we'll have all of our ropin events and end with barrels and poles! Let's get started! Up first we have Barren Davis ridin Ice Cold!" Rider after rider fell of only two boys rode the 8 and they were both newbies. "Now our broncs! Up first again is Barren Davis!" He rode the 8 but with terrible form. He got 81 points. A few riders went and Sawyer rode. Then Jacob rode the 8 and his score put him in first. Levi's score put him in second. "Up next we have Skylar Jones. What person names their son Skylar?" "They don't. They name their daughter Skylar!" Sky yelled as she climbed the fence. "Oh we have a lady out here! Good luck miss!" I'll show them! She thought. The horses name was Death by Fear. "Hey there bud. Ya never gonna throw me! I can ride anything! You go ahead and try your best, I ain't never comin off. Least till I win!" At that she nodded her head expecting the exploding left then immediate right. She rode the 8 with a score of 97 points. "Beat that suckers!" She yelled at the rest of the boys. "Let a lady show ya how to ride at I right? Up next we have...""That was cool!" Elena ran up to her friends. "Thanks! That was a fun ride!" Sky answered. "Let's go get ready for roping!" Levi shouted to the two girls. It was tie down now Levi, Elena, and Skylar rode and so far they were in third, first and second. Now Jacob was riding. He took off after the steer but as he was galloping his cinch came completely off. He somehow stayed in Magic but roped the steer in 17.847s. "What happened dude?" Levi was curious. "I don't know it just fell off!" He was pissed. They looked at the saddle and carved into the cinch was Sawyer. And the cinch strap was slashed three fourths of the way and ripped the rest. "Shit!"

"Next up is Levi Erickson riding Jazmin and Jacob Falterman riding Cowboy Magic." Levi and Jacob roped in 7s flat putting them in the lead. The girls were the last to go. They ran out Sky roped the head, pulled it around then Elena got both feet. 7s! "That's a tie ladies and gentlemen! 7s flat!" Now is barrels!In poles Skylar won to Elena with a time of 14.562s to 14.563s. Barrels went well with Skylar placing second due to a knocked barrel and Elena getting third for a slight pause before running home. "Not our best but we got in the top three." Ele sounded disappointed. "They did good!" Skylar said happily. "Girls come in here please!" Jacob yelled from inside the trailer. "What do y'all wa..." Sky stopped. "Why'd you tell them?!" She asked Elena. "I didn't they just knew!"She defended herself. "Let's party!" There were lots of people there, Barren and Dalia, Gregory and Taylor, Dalton, Bailey, Emily, Forest...all friends of the group. Dalia had become a good friend of theirs instead of an enemy. (Elena's POV)Jacob and I have been dancing for the past hour. It was the best until someone tripped me. I looked up and saw someone in a hood walking away fast. Jacob helped me up and I thanked him then we got a glass of water. "The party is great thank you!" "No problem. It's nothing for my bear!" We kissed and then went back to dancing.(Skylar's POV)The stench of alcohol, all the people. It was just like my last party. The only party my dad ever let me out of the closet for. My own party. People were yelling. They were happy yells of course but all I heard was my father. Flashback "You spilled your food! Your humiliating me in front of all my buddies! You shouldn't be out of your closet yet! You haven't learned your lesson obviously! Do you need your other punishment?!" "No daddy please! I'll be good I swear! I'll even clean up other people's spills!" "Other people don't spill! Only naughty children like you do! And where is my respect?!? You also didn't do your chores!" *slap* "I was in the closet daddy..." *cries* "you should have done them this morning! Aren't you waking up on time!!!???" "I get up at 6:30 daddy sir." "You are to wake up at 5:45 now since you can't get your simple chores done!" "Yes sir. Daddy? Sir?" "WHAT!" "If I get all my chores done can I not go in the closet please sir?" "We'll see if your good!"End flashbackI slowly backed into a corner away from everyone. A guy obviously drunk with a hood over his face started walking my way. "Hey there pretty thing! Why don't you come over and sit in daddy's lap?" His voice had little recognition but his drunken slur made it difficult to tell "No." "what did you say?" This whole scene was bringing back a flashback but I kept myself under control. "I said no." "Oh really? You are saying no? To me?" He got closer until he had me pushed against the wall. He pushed his knee between my legs. "No...means yes..." he started kissing my neck. There wasn't anything I could do he had his whole body pressed against me and was holding my hands. He was twice as strong as me and twice as big. "Yes mean harder..." he paused and then continued to kiss my squirming figure. Where is Levi! "The safe word is..." he bite my neck a little. "More." "Ok more!" "Ok i will." He was messing with me there was not safe word. When I tried to scream he took both my hands in one and covered my mouth. He was so close to me I couldn't even try kicking him. "Scream and you'll lose your innocence." He whispered in my ear. He let go of my mouth and ran his hand over my body. I screamed. "You piece of shit" I was going into another one of my daymares. Pretty much a panic attack. "Daddy stop! Don't touch me there!" "You don't tell me what to do brat!" He had raped me that day after my party. Not completely but enough to cause mental harm. I luckily still had my innocence. (Levi's POV)I heard a scream. It sounded like Skylar. "Skylar?!" I yelled out. I saw a guy slap her while pressing her against he wall with his body. "Get off her!" "Oh she likes it!" "It sure doesn't look like it! Plus that's my girl! Who are you?" I pulled of his hood and found out it was Sawyer. "Sawyer you ass! Get out!" I punched him multiple times before he passed out. Then I ran to Skylar who was having one of her panic attacks. I pulled her into my arms rubbed her back and sang her favorite song. It always works. She was soon asleep and I carried her to my bed. We lied there for and hour before she stirred. "Hey baby..." she screamed and fought to get away. "Hey hey Sky it's me Levi." I didn't hold her I let her get out of bed and turn and look at me. Then she started crying and ran back into my arms. "Let it out sweetheart. Let it out." "My dad raped me. Sorta. I'm still a virgin but he did enough to cause me trust issues and these panic attacks." "Baby I'm sorry I should have been watching you closer. I'm not ever leaving your side again. Your sleeping with me from now on ok?" "Ok."

Four Corners Part Two

We had drove to the next rodeo in the morning. It was in Denver, Colorado. The rodeo starts at 2, it isn't all that big so only a few hours. I mounted up on Honor and headed to the arena. We warmed up and pretty soon the whole squad was warming up. "Ladies and gentlemen! We start the 73rd annual Denver Round Up! First we're going to call out our ropers. We'll run teams then tie down and finally breakaway before intermission!" All the teams came out and got in line. Narrator POV"Next up we have Skylar Jones and Elena Lane!" They roped em down in 2.5s. "That's an arena record folks!" Levi and Jacob got 3.1s and second place. "Now let's tie down some steers!""Jacob Falterman riding Cowboy Magic!" He tied down in 4s flat. Putting him in the lead. ..."Levi Erickson riding Jazzi!" He got 4.1s. ..."Skylar Jones riding Honor!" She got 3.8s bumping Jacob to second. ... "And next is Elena Lane riding Hollywood Runner!"She got 3.9s putting her in third. Final results were Skylar; Elena; Jacob; Levi. ..."And now breakaway!"..."Levi Erickson riding Jazzi!" He got 3.1. ..."Skylar Jones riding Honor!" 2.9s..."Elena Lane on Hollywood Runner!" 2.8s..."Jacob Falterman riding Cowboy Magic!" 3.0sFin al results Elena, Skylar, Jacob, Levi."At intermission they got their horse and them selves some water and got changed for the next events.

"Let's get all our barrel racers out here shall we! First up Elena Lane riding Hollywood Runner!"She ran a 16.421s. ..."Next up we have Skylar Jones riding Honor!" Skylar's POV We ran through the gate and cut the first barrel. Perfect turn! We charged down the second and in no time we were baring down on the third. I asked for the turn and in those few seconds I saw Levi, in those same few seconds I felt it. Honor was going down. I heard the god awful noise come from his leg. He rolled over and my leg was stuck under him. I screamed in agony as we were going so fast we slid when he fell. We finally stopped moving completely and people had rushed over to help. "Skylar! Skylar! LET ME THROUGH YOU IDIOTS!" I heard Levi scream. "Bring me Levi please." I barely whispered. "Let him go!" The medic above me shouted. Levi ran over and put my head in his lap. He rubbed my hair and started singing my favorite song, Daddy's Boots by Dustin Lynch. Then I passed out.

Levi's POV (before the fall)She was just turning the third barrel. Our eyes connected, at that exact moment it happened. Honors leg bent and they went down. Skylar stayed with him like the great rider she is, but that came with a consequence. She is now stuck underneath him. They slid to a stop and I ran out to her. He guards stopped me but then a medic yelled to let me in. I ran to her and carefully placed her head on my lap. There I sung her favorite song. Then she went limp. "Skylar? Skylar!" I was terrified. Did she die?! Was she going to survive?! What about Honor?! All these thought we running through my head as I was pulled away from her almost in a trance. Medic POV "She went into shock then blacked out. She might have a head injury." I was barking out orders. When I saw the girl go limp I got worried but she was still breathing. We were all working on getting her out from under the horse when she started coming to. Skylar's POV I woke up lying on the arena ground. Then it all came back. Honor is still on top of me. My whole right leg is numb. I cannot feel it, I don't know if it's the adrenaline or if there is something wrong. Honor was screaming in pain and thrashing around trying to get up. "Hey boy. It's ok calm down." I whispered and cooed in his ear. He immediately stopped thrashing and lied still but he was still screaming. "Alright on three you lift and we'll pull. One...two...three!" I finally noticed the arms holding me. Many people lifted Honor up and other people drug me out. They lied me flat and started examining my leg. When I looked at it I knew immediately it was severely injured. I got up with the help of Levi and Jacob and they limped me out of the arena. I looked back one more time to look at Honor. Goodbye my baby! I will always love you! I thought to myself. Vet POV As I examine the leg it is completely shattered and cannot be fixed. I cut off some of his hair for Skylar and put him down. He was almost dead anyways. He had internal bleeds from the fall.

Four Corners Part Three

"Guys I can't believe that is how all this happened!" The group found out everything that happened to cause Skylar's accident. "God whoever did this is an ass! Sky could have been killed!" Elena was extremely upset. "Honor was killed!" Skylar cried. She could not believe her last connection to her mom was gone. "So what did they do?" Jacob asked as he was not there when they talked to the authorities. "Over the night they placed a board under the sand. They must know how close I come to the barrel (Closer than most because Honor could make the turn) But it was deep so it wouldn't be out of the sand enough until I or Elena rode." "Anyone could have found out the order." Levi commented.

Now their in Mt. Pleasant, Utah. It has been two weeks since the accident and Skylar will be riding Jazzi for barrel races. She can't participate in roping because you can't have two riders for the same horse. She has been searching for a new horse but hasn't found one yet that works. "Bronc riders please come behind the shoots." The announcer boomed over the speaker. "I signed up but should I ride?" Skylar was still worried about her leg. "If you want to." Elena said encouragingly. "No your not riding a Bronc." Levi said sternly but all out of love for her. "I think I'll scratch and sign up for the next one." She responded. "Good luck Levi! Love you!" "I love you too and thanks!" Levi ran off with Jacob. "Love you Ele!" Jacob yelled as he ran off. "Love you too Jacob." She said more to herself as she watched him go. "Let's head to the stands Sky!" "Ok." They walked to the grandstands and Ele placed her arm around Skylar. "Let go I can do this!" Elena backed off knowing Skylar is very independent. "Oh look Sky there's Levi!" Levi nodded and the gate flew open along with his horse. He rode well and received 98.796 points. Jacob got 98.998 points. "Nice job guys! First and Second!" "Thanks Elena! You guys better go get ready for barrels." Jacob suggested. "Ok!" Ele said excitedly. "I'll help you Skylar." Levi said happily. "Levi?" "Yes?" "I don't think I wanna race again..." "well why not? You've made it to the NFR. You are a very talented rider." "I'm just scared Levi!" "Well Jazzi will take good care of you. Just take this nice and slow." "Alright I will." "Next up Elena Lane ridin Hollywood Runner!" Elena ran a 15.764s run putting her in first place. Skylar is up. She rides up to the gate and asked Jaz for a canter. She did one circle then headed for the first barrel. She turned all three nice and leisurely, so she thought. "Skylar Jones riding Jazzi with a 17.129s putting her in fifth place! She's makin a comeback!" "Nice job!" "Thanks Jacob!" "You too Ele!" "Thanks babe!" "Let's go get ready for roping!" Levi shouted. "Away we go!" "I think I'm just goin to take a little nap in the trailer." Sky said pretending to be sleepy. "Ya no your not doin that." Levi whispered in her ear. "Urgh fine!" They all did well in breakaway and team roping. Elena was using Dalia as a partner for now. Now it's time for tie down. Mystery POV Slice here, a little cut here, and one final slice here. That'll doer. This will show them not to mess with me! Ha! I got one now it's time for the next. Elena's POV We shot out of the shoot and I roped my steer. I dallied off and went to step off. I got my leg just over Holly's back when *snap* my saddle slipped sideways and I face planted into the sand.

"Elena! Elena can you hear me?!" My ears were ringing and all the other sounds joined in. I heard spectators and medics. I opened my eyes and saw Jacob. He immediately kissed me and I saw he was crying.

Narrator POV Elena only had a concussion. She was fine, but everyone was shaken up. They all knew who did it.

None of them watched bull riding they all went straight to bed getting ready for the next rodeo.

Four Corners Part Four

On to the last rodeo before the NFR. It was August 1st. Tuscan Rodeo and Parade. They were now in Arizona. There was three days. The first holding Tie down and breakaway roping. The second holding broncs and bulls. And the third with barrels and team roping. Skylar is talking to Dalia bout usin a horse from her.

"His name's Sunny Cal. Called Sunny. He's a good all around geldin!" "Thanks Dalia! I owe ya!" "Ah it's no problem!" "See ya around!" "Bye now!"

"Next up we have Skylar Jones riding Sunny Cal!" "Let's go Sun!" Sky and Sunny whipped out of the shoot after their steer. She made sure to check her cinch right before she went. Now they were pulling to a stop as Sky leapt off her mount, flipped the steer, and tied him off. "Time!" She looked at the clock and saw 4.362s. "Yes! Good job Sunny!" She gave him a pat before trottin outta the arena. "Now can we have Elena Lane on Hollywood Runner?" "Let em rip Hollywood!" They bolted out and she had the steer before she was even out of the shoot. "Woooooweeee that was fast! 2.193s! So close to an arena record!" -a few riders- "Next up we'll have Levi Erickson riding Jazzi." He rode with a time of 4.591s. And Jacob rode in 4.726s. Elena won followed by Sawyer in second, Skylar with third, Levi with fourth, and finally Jacob in fifth. The group went back to the trailers for some lunch. "Hahaha that is the best! I can't wait to head back home for a while and we can all have a little break from all this chaos!" Jacob was laughing at a story Levi told about falling in a creek because his brother pushed him off a ledge. "Haha once when I was at my uncles we were all exploring," Skylar started telling her own story. "We were walking along and he stopped walking, 'Look there it's a bull frog!' He said with an evil smile on his face. I didn't pay any attention to it. He told me to catch it for him. It was on a really dry patch of dirt. So I thought. I went to run across it and sunk into the mud up to my waist! He was just laughing his butt off and so was everyone else!" Ele, Levi, and Jacob were on the ground laughing at the pictures Skylar showed them. *AN: this is a true story lol. He told me to run across it after the frog and I was naive enough to listen. It was a drained pond.* "Oh we're going to have so much fun together!!" Elena laughed. They continued telling each other stories over lunch, getting excited about going back home to Dallas.

Mystery POV

Alright what to do next? Hhhmmmm... I got it! Team roping I'm right before the girls! Little miss Hollywood isn't going to be so famous anymore! Hahahahahahahaha!

Narrator POV

"Time for breakaway folks! First up we have Jacob Falterman riding Cowboy Magic!" "Ok Magic get me close, and get me there fast! We got this!" They broke out at top speed and Jacob roped the black steer's horns, released the rope, and sat back. He finished in 3s. After a few riders it was Levi's turn to ride. He got a time of 3s as well. the girls went with Skylar getting 3.1s and Elena getting 2.9s."Hey Skylar!" "Yea Levi?" "Would you like to go to dinner tonight?" "That sounds great!" "Awesome! Dress nice we're going somewhere fancy!" "Ok! Yay!" "Jacob wanna go for a walk?" "Yea let's go!" "Geez there has been a lot of drama lately."Elena sighed. "I know there's to much excitement. Elena?" "Yes?" "Do you want to go on a date?" "Just me and you? That sounds really nice! We haven't done that!" "Alright great. Where do you wanna go?" "A pic-a-nick!"

They all headed back to the trailers to get dressed. "We're going on a real date. Just the two of us!" Elena swirled about. In her cute outfit.

"Levi and I are going out to dinner and then dancing. I know cliche but it's relaxing. And lord knows we need a break!" "Yea. I just hope nothing happens while we're out." "Same here. What should I wear? He said dress nice." "Hold on I got something for you!" She came out with a black and brown patterned dress. And Skylar added a pair of Ariat boots and a brown felt hat.

Narrator POV (focused on Skylar and Levi)"You ready Sky?" Levi shouted above the music in their trailer. "Yea one sec!" She walked out and over to Levi. "You look beautiful Skypie." "Thank you! You don't look to bad yourself!" She giggled. "I've never seen that dress is it new?" They we're talking on their way to the truck. "No it's Elena's." "Oh well it looks nice in you!" "Thank you." "Hi table for two?" "Yes please thank you." Levi answered and led the way. "What would you like to drink?" "I'll take a root beer please. And he'll have a 7up!" Skylar responded smiling for knowing her boyfriends answer. After the waitress walked away Levi giggled,"What if I wanted something different?" He joked. "Well it's to late for coffee and you really only drink 7up not much else." She smiled proudly. "I know. I'm just messin with you." They got their food and talked all the way through the meal. After paying and leaving a tip they headed off to the club. "Oh I love this song!" "Well...may I have this dance?" "Yes you may!" They slowly swayed to the music in each other's arms. "I love you Skypie!" "I love you to Blue Jeans!" "Hey what did you call me?!" "Blue Jeans!" "Why?" "Because your name is a brand of jeans." She said in a duh sort of tone. "You know what?" "What?" "I kinda like it!" "You do?" "Yea. Just don't call me that in front of the guys please." "Hmmmmm. I don't know. That's going to be really hard...ok I won't Blue Jeans." She smiled and pulled his head down for a kiss. (Earlier in the evening Elena's POV)Levi and Skylar just left for dinner when Jacob called me from outside the trailer. "Coming Jacob!" I grabbed my boots and hat and ran out the door. He had our horses tacked and was mounting up on Magic. "Where are going?" I asked for what felt like the hundredth time. "I'm not telling! It's a surprise!" Urgh he won't tell me! We have been riding toward the trees on the other side of the rodeo grounds. When we got to the trees I saw the most beautiful sight.

We walked through his pathway of lanterns to a creek with a little waterfall. It was overall amazing! At the creek was a blanket with he basket of food. Around the blanket was the little lanterns and a little pen for the horses. We untacked the horses, put them away and sat down on the blanket. We sat, ate, and talked all night. It was the best date ever!***The team decided to sleep in because bull riding was first today. They got up at 5am to feed then went back to bed until 10am. They got up and had breakfast: eggs, bacon, hash browns, and toast. Elena cooked and Skylar made the table while the guys did some cleaning up. Since they had eaten breakfast late, during lunch intermission they exercised the horses. Skylar and the guys all got ready for Bronc riding at 1pm. "Let's get our Bronc riders out here shall we?! First up is Jacob Falterman riding Nightmare." Jacob got on and rode great. All three made the eight and won first second and third;Skylar, Jacob, Levi. Next day"Next up is Team Skylar Jones and Elena Lane, horses Sunny and Hollywood Runner." They were sat back ready to go. When the buzzer rang they took off. Elena immediately felt something off but Holly didn't quite so she caught herself and roped the steer's head. Skylar grabbed the heels and dallied off earning them a time of 5.273s. "Nice job!" They have each other a high five and exited the arena. "Holly you ok?" She leaned down and pat her mount feeling her step off. "Let's just get back to the trailer and help the boys tack up." "Ok." They got over to the trailer and were astonished by what they saw. (Credit for this next section goes to Elena's POVAfter walking onto Sawyer holding a gun at Jacob, I lost it. "Why are you doing this?!! Huh!?""Well, look what the cats dragged in. Elena why don't you be a doll, and go fetch Jacob's horse??" " LIKE HECK I AM! I DON'T WORK FOR YOU, AND I'M NOT YOUR DOLL! YOU SHOULD LEAVE BEFORE SOMEONE ELSE WALKS UP AND CALLS THE COPS! " "ELENA! DO IT NOW!!! OR ELSE PRETTY HOLLYWOOD RUNNER GOES BYE BYE!" I walk over behind Jacob, and I grab Magic. "Bring him to me. NOW! " I walk up a little, then jump up on Magic and I kick him into a gallop. Magic runs off with me all the way to the other side of the arena. Police cars are there. I ride up to them. "Hello! I need some help!" "Yes, May I help you?" "My friends and our horses are in danger. My Ex boyfriend keeps plotting us, and he is over there with a gun at my boyfriend. Please come help!" The police gets on their horses, and follows Magic back to the spot. "HANDS UP WHERE WE CAN SEE THEM, PUT THE GUN DOWN SIR!" " I CAN'T! I NEED TO INJURY HER! " Sawyer says as he points to me.

Narrator's POVThe police hold their guns up at Sawyer. They shot at his fingers, and Sawyer drops the gun. The police walk up behind him, and cuff him. "Sir, you have the right to remain silent, for everything you say can, and will be used against you in a court of law. They put him in the cop car, and drive off towards the station. Elena walks Magic back to Jacob. "I love you so much, Ele. I'm glad that Sawyer is now behind bars." "I love you so much too, and I'm so glad he is behind bars too. " Elena helps untack Magic, while Levi hugs Sky. (End of 's part, thanks bud)

After all that Elena untacks Holly and starts grooming her. When she gets down to the bottom of her leg she finds why Holly was off.

"Oh Holly what happened!? Skylar!" "What wrong Ele?" "Holly's leg...it's got a cut. Her heel is cut off!" "Oh my!" Was all she said before calling the vet.--------------{}----------{}----------{}--------------"Oh my gosh I can believe we're finally going home!!" Elena shouted while packing her gear. "I know I miss you parents!" Skylar agreed. "So I've never asked but I guess I got my answer. You two live together?" Levi asked curiously. "No Skylar lives with her step mom and her half sister, her step mom divorced her dad after she moved in and found out what Maxwell was doing. But now that we're 18 we can move into the neighboring ranch. We've got some new colts and horses that need to be taken care of. Plus senior year!!"Elena was excited for her last year of high school. Skylar always loved the educational part of school but the social part she tried her best to avoid, because everyone knew about her history. "Yea surprisingly we have senior year too." Jacob said sadly. "Yay you can do it at our school!" Elena jumped into Jacob's arms and gave him a kiss. "I'd like it if you came to school with me." Skylar whispered in Levi's ear. "Would you now?" "Yes yes I would." "Well I'll just have to do it then." Levi smiled before leaning down and kissing Sky. Mmmmm was all Sky could say. "Love you Skypie." "Love you too Blue Jeans." "I love you Elena." Jacob kissed Elena's forehead softly. "I love you too Jacob."

Time for a Break

AN:This chapter is going to be long. Time frame: the month of August. "Omg Skylar!!!!!" "Sissy!!!! I've missed you so much!" "I'm to old for that nickname!" "Not from me! You'll never be to old for me to call you sissy!" Skylar hugged her sister, . "Who are they?" Maddi asked pointedly. "Oh this is Jacob Falterman and Levi Erickson." Skylar and Levi were holding hands and Maddi looked at Skylar accusingly. "Yes he's my boyfriend and no you can not give him the sister talk." Skylar laughed at her sisters face. "Awww! Well here's the short version. Don't you ever hurt her or I can make your death look like an accident. I already did for our dad." She gave an evil smile then a cute crooked smile, winked and skipped away. Maddi just turned 17 but she was still able to skip while looking cute. "Come inside guys lunch is ready!" "Ok let us just slip the horses in the pasture!" Elena yelled back.

Everyone was sitting around the table eating grilled cheese with some fruit. Everyone including: the squad, Elena's parents; Garret and Luaren, Skylar's stepmom; Erin, Maddi, and Elena's 10 year old sister, Kourtney. "Where are your parents at boys?" Luaren asked. "My parents are at our 50 acre farm about 3 miles away from here. I'll be checkin in with them tomorrow." Jacob replied. "Oh that's good!" Luaren smiled. "What about you Levi?" "I'll be headed down to my parent's ranch tomorrow." "Where's your place at son?" Garret asked Levi. "Oh it's actually on the backside of the girls' ranch!" "That's great so your just back that way?" "Yes ma'am we are." Levi smiled at Erin. "Well how bout y'all go care for the horses." Garret told the kids. Maddi and Kourt led the gang around showing them all the horses. "Here's the new stock."

"We have Rosie, Crystal, Cowboy, Daisy, Blue, Ember, and Annie." "Blue is beautiful!" Elena said her mouth practically on the ground.

"Yes he was one of the better ones to train. Dad likes him says he's got heart and spirit but kind and gentle. Best kind of horse." Kourtney smiled. "And this is Ember right?" Skylar asked. "Yea that's Ember, or Ivy Fox is her official name. Momma says she has the same sire as Honor!" Maddi replied.

"Well I might be trying her on the barrels. She looks like an appendix." "Momma thought you'd like her. And yea she is! She had me try her a few times. She's fantastic! With you trainin her you'll win the NFR no doubt about it!" Maddi pet Ember's forehead. "Well I'll take a look at her info later on. Let's get on with feedin why don't we?" Skylar took off for the feed room. "Since y'all don't know the grain mixtures y'all can give out the hay. Breeders get two flakes, and it says on their stall door name plate." Kourtney says to everyone. "Alrighty sounds good." Levi said while joining Skylar in the feed room. Skylar's POV

"Alright let's see if I can find your papers Ember. Here's the filing cabinet for papers. Geez I forgot how much stuff is in here. Ok Ivy...Ivy...Ivy...where are you Ivy?" "What ya doin?" "AH OUCH! Why'd you do that!" He snuck up behind me and I had my head in the filing cabinet. When he said that he spooked me and I smacked my head on the top. "Hahaha oh Sky I'm...hahaha... sorry. Are you ok?" He was laughing but he really was worried. "Yea I'm ok. Im trying to find Ember, or Ivy's, information...Ah there it is!" I grabbed her papers and sat down at the desk. "Wow this is a nice horse. I see why Garret bought her." I said more to myself than to Levi but he still responded. "What's she got in her?" "In her dam's side she's all quarter with Doc, Bar, and Leo. And her sire's side is all thoroughbred with Bold Ruler, meaning she's related to Secretariat, her grandsire is his brother." "Nice!" I grabbed her papers and his hand and we headed inside. "So what do you think of Ember?" Garret asked me eyeing the papers in my hand. "She's beautiful. And has amazing bloodlines. I'll try her on the barrels in the next week or so. Mainly cause I got nothin much else to do." "Well there's always horses to ride round here!" Luaren laughed while brining in the food for dinner. "So you girls goin to get your stuff moved over to your ranch house?" Erin asked. "Yea the guys are goin to help us after dinner." Elena said happily. "Good. You boys going to move in too?" Luaren asked suggestively. "Yea I think we will for the next few months." Levi said with a large smile. "You all ready for senior year!" Maddi said in a sing song voice. "Ugh." Was all we said. Later that evening "Hey Skylar?" "Yes Garret?" "I have a few things for you!" "Ok one second!" She set down her box in the trailer and walked inside the barn. Standing there was a silver dun gelding with a beautiful tack set on him. On his halter was a name plate that read Silver with Sily in smaller letters underneath. "Oh he's beautiful Garret! And the tack! Unbelievable!" "I'm glad you like it Skylar! And Ember is yours. Here's her new halter!" The halter was red and black with little beads and with her name plate on it: Ivy Fox and underneath Ember. "Thank you so much. I love it!" She gave him a hug then took her new horses to the trailer. "Hey baby!" "Hey mom! Wassup?" Well I got you a little something for Ember." "Really?!" "Yeah it's here in this box and the rest is in the tack room I sent Levi to go get it." "Oh wow it's amazing! How did you ever find something like this?!" "I came across it at an auction!" "I love it! Thank you mom!" "Your welcome sweetie!"

"Elena!" "Yes daddy?" "Here ya go!" "Oh my gosh! Blue is mine?!" "Yes he is!" "Oh thank you thank you thank you!!!" She loaded Blue into the trailer. Then the gang headed to the ranch house.

"Wow girls this place is awesome!" Jacob and Levi were in awe. "Thanks! We're so excited to live here! And to have you here too!" Elena jumped up the stairs. They had already unloaded all their horses and tack and now started on the house. They completely unpacked their stuff into the house and they all headed up to bed.

Senior Year Begins

School starts tomorrow and I'm so not ready. I always have a panic attack on the first day because someone brings up my past. *flashback*I was just about to walk into my first period when someone pushed me against the lockers. "Hey there pretty thing! You free tonight?" Before I could respond he cut in again."Of course your free. You'd do anything to get with someone besides your dad, or so you saayyy..." The tears started to fall and he pushed me again. " Look at me when we're talking! Come here babe." He pulled me in to kiss me but I pushed him off and ran for Elena. The walls were closing in and I couldn't breath, I was being suffocated. *end flashback*But this year I have Levi. He will help me through everything. I am always popular because of Elena but being popular means everyone knows you and your secrets get out fast. But now I'd be the second most popular girl with the hottest boyfriend! I thought as I looked at Levi sitting beside me on the couch. We were all watching movies to try and relax before tomorrow. So not working for me!

Narrator POV The gang drove to school at 7:30 in the morning and parked in Skylar and Elenas' spot right in front. "So are you girls the popular chicks everyone moves for?" Jacob asked as they were getting out of the truck. "They do even though we've never asked them to. We just GET this spot and just GET out lunch table, which btw has a bunch of people you guys will love!" Elena said while jumping up on the tailgate, they were early like usual waiting for the rest of the group. "Hey Megan, Jaimie! This is Levi and Jacob!" Skylar greeted the couple. "Hey there newbies! How'd you get in our group on the first day?" Jaimie asked while letting go of Megan's hand to shake the guys' "We just so happen to be their boyfriends." Levi responded laughing and shaking Jaimie's hand. "Oooooohhh Skylar! Elena! Y'all found yourselves some nice cowboys?" Megan whispered. "Hahahaha! Yes we did and they're lovely!" Elena and Skylar said at the same time. "I love you!" Skylar leaned over and whispered in Levi's ear then pulling him down and kissing him. "Ooooooooohhh!" Said a new voice. "Payton! My girl!" Elena squealed then ran over and hugged the short girl. Jacob's POV A short girl with platinum blonde hair and bright blue eyes walked up and cooed at Skylar as she kissed Levi. Next thing I know, right as I was about to kiss Elena she squealed and hugged the new girl whose name must be named Payton, she screamed that as she jumped up. Four other people walked up, another girl with red hair and freckles across her nose and cheeks, also a boy who looked just like her. They must be siblings. Behind them is two guys, one with brown hair and green eyes, the other with dark brown eyes and hair. "Hey Emma, Dalton." Skylar said as the red heads walked up. "Austin! Riley! There you guys are! Guys this is Jacob, my boyfriend..." Elena pointed to me then Levi."...and Levi, Skylar's boyfriend!" "Nice to meet y'all." Levi said and I shook their hands. Then the bell rang and we all went to first period, surprisingly we all had sports conditioning. Afterwards Skylar, Levi, and I have English, while Elena and the others have government. Elena and I have Spanish 4 together after that while Skylar and Levi have math. And so on with the fun school day (note the sarcasm).Levi's POV It's time for third period and I am walking with Sky to our math class. We walk in and I follow her to sit near the window. She must like to day dream out that, and I see why there is a field of horses. "Well hello there Skylar!" A young woman with hazel eyes and brown hair with blonde highlights walks up to Sky. She must be another friend of hers. "Hey here Fryster!" Yup must be a friend. "How's my favorite student?" Ok maybe not a friend! " I'm doin well. How's my favorite teacher?" "I am fantastic and the boys they can't wait till they can come into class with me!" "Oh I can't wait to see them again. By the way this is Levi Erickson, new student and my boyfriend!" Skylar motioned to me and I stepped forward to shake her hand. "Well it's nice to meet you Levi, my name is Mikel Frye." "Very nice to meet you too, Mrs. Frye!" "So Skylar how's the rodeoing going?" "Well it was going great until a horrible accident that ended up killing Honor." I wrapped her in my arms enough to comfort her but not enough to disturb the convo. "Oh I'm so sorry to hear that! Have you found a replacement for the NFR?" " How do you know about that?" "The whole school knows about you and Elena. NFR for barrel racing and roping. And you for Bronc riding." "Wow I didn't know the news got around so fast!" "Well it was in the news! 'Local Dallas girls make it to NFR rodeo for barrel racing! And one of the girls is nominated best rider of the year for Bronc riding in the Finals Rodeo!'" "Oh my gosh that's crazy!" *Ding* "Alright that's time gotta start class! Hey there students!" "Hey Fryster!" I have never seen a class so enthusiastic! This should be a fun class!

*After School*The gang got up on the horses and rode out to check on their cattle. They were almost to the ridge when they herd a couple whinnies. They went around the corner and found four little foals, and one was tangled in some rope.

Skylar walked up to the young colt to calm it down. She then moved to the hind foot to untangle it from the rope. As soon as she got the rope off it jumped up and stood by the others. There was one grey, one blue roan, one red roan, and the one that was caught was a very light palomino. She walked back to Silver to grab the ropes she carried and distributed them between her now dismounted friends. "Where do they come from?" Levi asked. "I don't know. Maybe they're wild and lost their herd." Skylar responded. "I think I remember seeing a herd a couple times while I was out with my dad looking after the cattle." Elena thought back a few years. "Well should we take them home?" Jacob asked hopefully. "Well yea we should so they're safe." Skylar got Silver grazing and started walking toward the grey colt. They slowly crept up to the colts cooing to them as they do. They made makeshift rope halters and tied it to their saddles then headed up the hill to finish what they started. They counted cattle and calves and rode slowly back to the house. When they got there they took the foals to the round pen by the barn. They tied up the foals and started working on grooming them. After working with the foals a little they all had a name for the foal they chose. "I'm gonna name him Bear!" Elena said giving Bear a quick kiss on the muzzle. "You'll be Encore!" Skylar whispered in her fuzzy ear. "Buddy!" Levi announced. "This will be Bonus. Because he's my Bonus horse!" "Awesome! Now let's get them in the front pasture and feed them." Elena said and took her colt to the pasture, followed by the Sky, Levi, and Jacob. They had dinner and did their homework before finishing up chores and working with a few of the two year olds they got from Elena's parents. Then they took showers and went to bed.

The Calm Before The Storm

Skylar and Elena went out shopping for clothes, much to Sky's arguments. After shopping for a few hours they had everything they needed. "Are we done yet? My feet hurt!" Skylar was done with shopping an hour ago. "Yup! Now let's go home for some lunch!" They drove home and made BLT's for them and the boys who had been cleaning the whole barn. "We'll do the pastures. After food!" "You and food, Elena!" "That's right! I love food!" "Same here Ele!" "Oh Skypie, Elena, your love for food is just after your love for horses." Levi and Jacob laughed. "Noooo! It's after you, after horses!" Skylar argued. "Awww you love me more than food! I feel special!" Levi pulled Skylar into a hug from behind and kissed her cheek. "Yes I do. Horses are always first but your a very close second." "Well I feel honored! Now your done eating so time for pastures!" Levi poked her in the side to shoo her out the door. Jacob doing the same to Elena.

"So we gonna go to that old cabin?" "Oh Levi it's gonna be great! I hope Elena likes her gift..." "Of course she will Jacob! I'm not so sure about Skylar though... She's not one for jewelry. I've never seen her wear any besides that small horseshoe necklace. And on dates she has earrings sometimes." "Oh stop she'll love it!" "If you think so."

"Ugh I hate cleaning the pastures! It's too hot!" "Oh Elena stop complaining at least there's the creek right there that I can do this with!" Skylar shoved Elena into the water. "Ahhhh that was NOT! NICE!" Elena screamed. "Nope but it was funny!" "Whatever! We're done let's head inside!"

"Hey y'all wanna go riding?" Jacob called from the kitchen. " Yeah! Where we headed?" Elena asked. "Well it's Friday and a four day weekend so I thought we'd go on a little trip before training hard." He shrugged. "Ok sounds great!" "Alright I've got everything packed and Levi has the horses tacked! All we have to do is put the packs on the horses." "Alright let's get on it!" Elena and Jacob joined Skylar and Levi.

Elena rode Blue, Levi rode Jazzi, Jacob was on Magic, and Skylar rode Ember. They all took off down the trail for their weekend adventure! "This is a beautiful trail Jacob!" "Yea how do you know about this?" "Remember I used to live right backed to y'all!" "Oh..." "Yea me and my dad used to take this all the time!" "That's cool!" They laughed and rode on until 9:00pm when it finally got dark there they stopped at an oak tree and camped the night. They lit a little fire, tied the horses in some grass, and set out their blankets. After eating dinner they all went to sleep. They woke up early and ate breakfast. At about 11:30 the gang made it to the lake. They set up a little camp and put the horses in a conveniently placed corral. Jacob and Elena went off fishing while Levi and Skylar went swimming. Jacob's POV We walked over to my favorite spot to cast out. It always had the biggest and most fish. Also it was the most beautiful spot on the lake. We have been fishing for an hour now and we are sitting next to each other talking away. "It's beautiful!" "You're beautiful!" "Aw thank you! Your not too bad yourself!" Elena laughed and I couldn't help but laugh with her. "Elena...I have been putting this off for who knows what reason. But I wanted to give you this." I held out the promise ring in my hands.

"Oh Jacob! Wha...what is this?" She was stunned. "It's just a promise ring! Don't worry. Ele I love you very much and wanted to make sure you knew that." "Thank you." She whispered in my ear. I leaned in and kissed her passionately. We fished for a few more hours before heading back.(wrote this part)Levi and Skylar cuddle on the beach and look at the clouds. After a few minutes they sit in silence. Levi kisses her cheek and places the present in her hands. Skylar's POV: Levi just gave me a long, wrapped box. I wonder whats in it. i start to unwrap it, and open the box. *jaw dropped* "I LOVE IT!!

I take out a gorgeous Emerald necklace with matching Earrings. "Im glad you love it." "I love you, Levi!" "I love you too, Sky!" Elena and Jacob rode up, as Sky and Levi were leaving. "Wanna ride back now?" I ask them. "SURE, we were just heading out to find y'all!" Elena said. Elena and Jacob turned the horses around, and rode back with Sky and Levi to the house. Narrator's POV: They got back to the house, and Sky and Levi made lunch. Peanut butter and Jelly Sandwich.

Everyone ate, and Elena and Jacob went to their room, and started to watch season 12 of supernatural. *beep-beep* Elena's phone went off, and a reminder from her calendar pops up. * September 18: Jacob's Birthday!* Elena smiles, realising today was September 17, and she gets an idea in her head.(End of part)That evening they fed the ten horses they had as of now, Ember, Silver, and Encore are Sky's. Hollywood, Blue, and Bear are Ele's. Jazzi and Bonus are Levi's, finally Magic and Buddy are Jacob's. Everyone took care of their own horses unless one of them was inside doing something along the lines of dinner, homework, or cleaning, then they would help them out.

Parties and Training

Elena's POV I've been talking to Skylar about Jacob's Surprise party and we have all the details. It will be tonight in the hay barn at 6:00pm. We have a bunch of friends helping set it up. We're lighting a bonfire and there's a creek in the dark to have a little fun . But my present for him is my favorite! I got him a dog tag with a special engraving on it. "Elena? Are you still on planet earth?" Oops my English teacher caught me daydreaming. "Yes I'm here." "Ok what is the quote I just told the class?" My lap vibrated and I looked at my phone, Jacob had sent me a text about the answer. "Today is only one day in all the days that will ever be. But what will happen in all the other days that ever come can depend on what you do today. Ernest Hemingway." I smiled at her and continued doodling, or so she thought. E- Thanks Bae!<3J- NP ;p <3 what were you thinking about anyways?E- Just stuff...J- Ah sure... she's looking, talk after class :*<3E- Kk :*<3The bell rang and we went to lunch. "Hey look who decided to show up!" Jaimie commented causing everyone to laugh. "Hey let's all hang at our place tonight!" Skylar announced raising her water bottle. "Yeah!" I agreed. After school we got to the house and got dressed for the party. Skylar and I are choosing each other's dresses for the party. I have no idea what she has in store for me. She walked out with a deep purple knee length dress, the dress had a sequined belt and shoulder straps. The dress was tight fitting on the top and was loose at the skirt. I put it on with my brown Ariats and went to choose her outfit. I looked through our combined dresses and found a beautiful light blue high-low with a metallic inner skirt and a swirling sequined belt, it was a strapless. I brought out her white cross Ariats and her special black felt hat. When I showed her the outfit she actually smiled and looked genuinely excited to put it on. We got dressed then went to see the guys. Guys picking out fits in Jacob's POV We didn't dress super fancy just a simple pearl snap and wranglers, along with boots and hats. My shirt was a purple-black color with black pearls. Levi wore a black shirt with blue stitching and blue pearls. After slipping our hats on we walked to the living room and waited for the girls to get ready. The girls came out and we escorted them out to the horses. I know we are having a double date for my birthday at the hay barn because we are low and need to get a new load. We rode out to the barn, giant shed with a large round pen for the horses, Levi and I offered to take care of all the horses. Levi finished before me and went inside, when I was done I walked to the side door. When I opened the door all our friends yelled,"Surprise!" I jumped but laughed and hugged Elena when she came over. **They danced all night to their favorite songs, everything was great! Then the door opened again. Everyone looked over to see who the late show was,

Ele and Sky almost started crying at the sight. "Well well well! What is this? A party? It can't be for miss Ele...or Skypie so it's got to be for Jacob or Levi." Sawyer smiled his crazy smile. "Sawyer leave before you get hurt!" Jacob said stepping in front of Ele. "I'm not going anywhere!" He pulled out a knife. "Your barn is already burning so don't worry about saving your horses!" Sky and Ele started running for the back door. "Get back here! You won't get away!" Jacob and Levi grabbed Sawyer and ripped the knife out of his hands. Then they hog tied him and called the police.

Skylar and Elena ran out to jump on the horses they rode here then galloped back to the barn. There they grabbed a hose and put out the hay fire before it destroyed anything other than the feed room. Which was in need of a restock anyways. They checked all the horses and headed back to the party to find the cops taking Sawyer back to jail.

The rest of the party went smoothly, they opened presents, had cake, and played games. At about one am everyone finally went home.

One week laterThe girls and guys have been practicing nonstop for the upcoming NFR. They have a tight schedule with school, friends, practice, and keeping the property together. But somehow they make it all work.

Nation Finals Rodeo

December 8 We arrived at the rodeo grounds in Las Vagas and they were spectacular! I couldn't believe how big the grounds were! I unloaded Ember and took her over to a small arena to lunge her, just to stretch her legs. If I let her loose she'll roll and we have a race in two hours.

"Can we get all our Bronc riders please?" The announcer boomed. I went over to draw my horse. It was Knightshade again, yay (note the sarcasm). I climbed in the shoot giving him my normal down talk to make him mad as hell then nodded and slapped his ass. He shot straight up hen turned out, he threw me his worst and hardest bucks but it was like I was glued there on his back. I didn't even notice the buzzer went off until the pick up rider came over to ask if I was stuck. I shook my head and let him help me off. I ran over to Levi and Elena to hug them then Elena and I went to get ready for roping. We placed very well in roping earning very high scores giving us a better shot at overall. "Alright barrel racers! Let's see some action from the main attraction!" Elena was before me. I was terrified, this would be my first competition on Ember. And it was the NFR! I watched as Elena ran for the first making a picture perfect turn and runnin got the second. Her second was even better if that was even possible. Then her third! I don't know how but she got even closer to that barrel but didn't even nudge it! It was amazing. She got 15.397s! "Omg! Fantastic job Ele!" I hugged her before she even got off her horse. After seven more riders I was up. I rode up to the shoot as the last rider came out. I leaned forward and whispered in Ember's ear," Be my wings and I'll be your eyes!" Then I encouraged her forward to her first barrel. I asked for the turn and she gave it. We were so close to that barrel I'm surprised it is still standing. The second I could feel it brush my jeans. I gotta watch her in this one. She got close enough for my boot to tap the barrel but it didn't budge. We ran home like there was no tomorrow. I hope tomorrow is just like this!

It is! Today Ember is just like yesterday! So is Elena and Holly! We happened to have times off by one thousandth of a second. I got 15.396s. Today is the determining day! I got first on broncs, Elena won tie down and break away, the guys beat us in team. And now is barrels again. The times were so close for Elena and I that they had to go down two more numbers. I got 15.12643s and Elena got 15.12642! We are so close to each other it's amazing. I don't know what they don't just call it a tie. It's time for final awards. Levi won overall cowboy and Jacob got runner up. They tied for Grand Champions for tie down and beat us in team, they didn't win but they beat us. For break away Elena got Second and me third. Elena got barrel Grand Champion after our average times! And I won overall cowgirl because of my Bronc riding! In the end my first NFR rodeo was the best and most memorable day of my life, because as I was going up to receive my Overall Cowgirl award Levi met me up there and proposed!

CPSIA information can be obtained
at www.ICGtesting.com
Printed in the USA
LVHW030755211122
733624LV00009B/1049